WORDS AND THEIR MEANINGS

Aldous Huxley

WORDS AND THEIR MEANINGS

PUBLISHED AND DISTRIBUTED BY:
RIT Press
90 Lomb Memorial Drive
Rochester, New York 14623

ISBN 978-1-939125-45-3

LIBRARY OF CONGRESS CATALOGING-IN-PUBLICATION DATA
Names: Huxley, Aldous, 1894–1963, author.
Title: Words and their meanings / Aldous Huxley.
Description: Rochester, New York : RIT Press, [2018]
Identifiers: LCCN 2018009160 | ISBN 9781939125453 (print (hardcover) : alk. paper)
Subjects: LCSH: Meaning (Psychology) | Psycholinguistics.
Classification: LCC BF463.M4 H88 2018 | DDC 401—dc23
LC record available at https://lccn.loc.gov/2018009160

DECORATIONS BY ALVIN LUSTIG

FOREWORD

While I was browsing the shelves of a favorite used bookstore in Woodstock, Vermont, a peculiar title caught my attention: *Words and Their Meanings* seemed an ambitious subject for such a slender volume. Curiosity piqued, I pulled the book from the shelf and began reading. The intimacy of Aldous Huxley's text was magnetic. It was as though I was eavesdropping on a private tutorial. Turning pages yielded the experience that only rarely occurs when reading someone else's words, a complete understanding of something long felt but not previously expressed. Huxley's text brought clarity to something I had been thinking about but had not articulated—along with the recognition that I had been taking words for granted.

My career is in the "words business." Initially in the printing industry and now in marketing, I help businesses create belief in their ideas through the development and dissemination of language. For more than a decade, much of my work involved technology. A continuous stream of software and new online tools steadily disrupted antiquated marketing strategies and channels. Marketers responded by looking for any innovation that promised to deliver their message more effectively. Standing in the bookstore's aisle, reading Huxley's seventy-five-year-old words, I realized we were missing the point. The magic of belief is created by the words we choose to amplify, not by the method of amplification.

Leaving Vermont with a signed first edition of *Words and Their Meanings* and a new perspective on my work, I was driven to read everything I could find about the current science on language and belief. With my clients, conversation about message delivery technology was now pushed back so the harder work of message development could come first. Now a convert, I wanted to share Huxley's wisdom with peers and clients, but an online search for additional copies of the book turned up only one: another signed first edition—and appropriately priced. Revisiting the book's colophon,

I read, "100 copies of *Words and Their Meanings* have been specially printed for Jake Zeitlin." This was going to be a difficult book to share.

I am fortunate to have friends at RIT Press. When I first approached Bruce Austin, the Press's director, about reproducing Huxley's book, he immediately recognized the design of Alvin Lustig, whose archive was donated to RIT's Cary Graphic Design Archive. Bruce shared my enthusiasm for reintroducing the title and, through the Press, secured permission from Ritchie, the Huxley and Lustig estates to reproduce the copy you now hold.

In one conversation about *Words and Their Meanings*, we discussed the context in which it was written. In the spring of 1940, much of the world had "progressed" from a war of words to a war of arms—a point Huxley notes. Closing the essay, Huxley warns about the misuse of words: "they are matters of the profoundest ethical significance to every human being." As this foreword is written, in a time rife with accusations of fake news and claims to alternative facts, Huxley's text is well worth revisiting. It is, in fact, timeless.

Jon Budington
President, More Vang
January 2018

WORDS AND THEIR MEANINGS

Words and their meanings—this is the subject I have chosen. Some of you, no doubt, will wonder at my choice; for the subject will strike you as odd and unimportant, even rather silly. This is quite understandable. For a long time past, thinking men have tended to adopt a somewhat patronizing attitude towards the words they use in communicating with their fellows and formulating their own ideas. "What do you read, my lord?" Polonius asked. And with all the method that was in his madness Hamlet scornfully replied, "Words, words,

words." That was at the beginning of the seventeenth century; and from that day to this the people who think themselves realists have gone on talking about words in the same contemptuous strain.

There was a reason for this behaviour—or at least an excuse. Before the development of experimental science, words were too often regarded as having magical significance and power. With the rise of science a reaction set in, and for the last three centuries words have been unduly neglected as things having only the slightest importance. A great deal of attention has been paid, it is true, to the technical languages in which men of science do their specialized thinking, particularly, of course, to mathematics. But the colloquial usages of everyday speech, the literary and philosophical dialects in which men do their thinking about the problems of morals, politics, religion and psychology—these have been strangely neglected. We talk about 'mere matters of words' in a tone which implies that we regard words as things beneath the notice of a serious-minded person.

This is a most unfortunate attitude. For the fact is that words play an enormous part in our lives and are therefore deserving of the closest study. The old idea that words possess magical powers is false; but its falsity is the distortion of a very important truth. Words *do* have a magical effect—but not in the way that the magicians supposed, and not on the objects they were trying to influence. Words are magical in the way they affect the minds of those who use them. "A mere matter of words," we say contemptuously, forgetting that words have power to mould men's thinking, to canalize their feeling, to direct their willing and acting. Conduct and character are largely determined by the nature of the words we currently use to discuss ourselves and the world around us. The magician is a man who observes that words have an almost miraculous effect on human behaviour and who thinks that they must therefore be able to exercise an equal power over inanimate nature. This tendency to objectify psychological states and to project them, thus objectified, into the external world is deeply rooted in the human mind. Men have made this mistake in the past, men are making it now; and the results are invariably deplorable. We owe to it not only the tragic fooleries of black magic, but also (and this is even more disastrous) most of the crimes and lunacies committed in the name of religion, in the name of patriotism, in the name of political and economic ideologies. In the age-long process by which men have consistently stultified all their finest aspirations, words have played a major part. It was, I believe, the realization of this fact that prompted the founders of the two great world religions to insist upon the importance of words. In the Christian gospels the reference to this matter is contained in one of those brief and enigmatic sayings which, like so many of the *logia*, unfortunately lend themselves to a great variety of interpretations. “But I say unto you, that every idle word that men shall speak, they shall give account thereof in the day of judgment. For by thy words thou shalt be justified, and by thy words thou shalt be condemned.” It is possible to interpret this utterance in terms of a merely magical theory of the significance of language. It is equally possible to put another construction on the saying and to suppose that what Jesus was referring to was what may be called the psychological magic of words, their power to affect the thinking, feeling and behaviour of those who use them. That it was the intention of the Buddha to warn men against such psychological magic the surviving documents leave us in no doubt whatever. ‘Right speech’ is one of the branches of the Buddhist’s Eightfold Path; and the importance of restraint in the use of words for intellectual purposes is constantly stressed in all those passages in the Pali Scriptures, where Gotama warns his followers against entangling themselves in the chains of metaphysical argument.

It is time now to consider a little more closely the mechanism by which words are able to exercise their psychological magic upon the minds of men and women. Human beings are the inhabitants, not of one universe, but of many universes. They are able to move at will from the world, say, of atomic physics to the world of art, from the universe of discourse called 'chemistry' to the universe of discourse called 'ethics'. Between these various universes philosophy and science have not as yet succeeded in constructing any bridges. How, for example, is an electron, or a chemical molecule, or even a living cell related to the G Minor quintet of Mozart or the mystical theology of St. John of the Cross? Frankly, we don't know. We have no idea how thought and feeling are related to physical events in a living brain and only the very vaguest notions about the way in which a brain is related to the charges of electrical energy which appear to be its ultimate components. So far as we are concerned, the only connection between these various universes consists in the fact that we are able to talk about all of them and in some of them to have direct intuitions and sensuous experiences. The various universes we inhabit all belong to *us*; that is the only thing that unites them. Logical and scientific bridges are non-existent; when we want to pass from one to another, we have to jump.

Now, all these various universes in which we live are members of one or other of two super-universes; the universe of direct experience and the universe of words. When I look at this paper in my hand I have a direct sensuous experience. If I choose to, I can keep my mouth shut and say nothing about this experience. Alternatively, I may open my mouth and, making use of a certain systems of signs, called the English language, I may impart the information that my experience consisted of whiteness mitigated by rows of black marks which I recognize as belonging to the alphabetical system by means of which spoken language can be rendered in terms of a visible equivalent.

To discuss the formal mechanism by which the world of immediate human experience is related to the various languages of mankind is a task which, even if I had the time, I should be quite incompetent to perform. And fortunately it is not necessary for our present purposes that it should be performed. It is enough, in this context, to point out that, between the world of immediate experience and the world of language, between things and words, between events and speech, certain relations have in fact been established; and that these relations are governed by rules that are in part purely arbitrary, in part dictated by the nature of our common experiences. The form of the rules varies from language to language. We are not, however, concerned with these variations. For our present purposes, the significant fact is that all human societies use some kind of language and have done so from the remotest antiquity.

Human behaviour as we know it, became possible only with the establishment of relatively stable systems of relationships between things and events on the one hand and words on the other. In societies where no such relationship has been established, that is to say, where there is no language, behaviour is nonhuman. Necessarily so; for language makes it possible for men to build up the social heritage of accumulated skill, knowledge and wisdom, thanks to which it is possible for us to profit by the experiences of past generations, as though they were our own. There may be geniuses among the gorillas; but since gorillas have no conceptual language, the thoughts and achievements of these geniuses cannot be recorded and so are lost to simian posterity. In those limited fields of activity where some form of progress is possible, words permit of progress being made.

Nor is this all. The existence of language permits human beings to behave with a degree of purposefulness, perseverance and consistency unknown among the other mammals and comparable only to the purposefulness, perseverance and consistency of insects acting under the compulsive force of instinct. Every instant in the life, say, of a cat or a monkey tends to be irrelevant to every other instant. Such creatures are the victims of their moods. Each impulse as it makes itself felt carries the animal away completely. Thus, the urge to fight will suddenly be interrupted by the urge to eat; the all-absorbing passion of love will be displaced in the twinkling of an eye by a no less absorbing passion to search for fleas. The consistency of human behaviour, such as it is, is due entirely to the fact that men have formulated their desires, and subsequently rationalized them, in terms of words. The verbal formulation of a desire will cause a man to go on pressing forward towards his goal, even when the desire itself lies dormant. Similarly, the rationalization of his desire in terms of some theological or philosophical system will convince him that he does well to persevere in this way. It is thanks to words and to words alone that, as the poet says:

> Tasks in hours of insight willed
> May be in hours of gloom fulfilled.

And let us remember incidentally that by no means all of our tasks are willed in hours of insight. Some are willed in hours of imbecility, some in hours of calculating self-interest, some under the stress of violent emotion, some in mere stupidity and intellectual confusion. If it were not for the descriptive and justificatory words with which we bind our days together, we should live like the animals in a series of discrete and separate spurts of impulse. From the psychological point of view, a theology or a philosophy may be defined as a device for permitting men to perform in cold blood and continuously actions which, otherwise, they could accomplish only by fits and starts and when the impulse was strong and hot within them. It is worth remarking, in this context, that no animals ever make war. They get into individual squabbles over food and sex; but they do not organize themselves in bands for the purpose of exterminating members of their own species in the name of some sacred cause. The emphasis here must be placed on the word 'name.' For, of course, animals have no lack of sacred causes. What could be more sacred to a tiger than fresh meat or tigresses? What is lacking in the animal's world is the verbal machinery for describing and justifying these sacred causes. Without words, perseverance and consistency of behaviour are, as we have seen, impossible. And without perseverance in slaughter and consistency in hatred there can be no war.

For evil, then, as well as for good, words make us the human beings we actually are. Deprived of language we should be as dogs or monkeys. Possessing language, we are men and women able to persevere in crime no less than in heroic virtue, capable of intellectual achievements beyond the scope of any animal, but at the same time capable of systematic silliness and stupidity such as no dumb beast could ever dream of.

It is time now that I gave a few typical instances of the way in which words have power to modify men's thought, feeling and conduct. But before doing so, I must make a few more remarks of a general nature. For our present purposes, words may be divided into three main classes. The first class consists of words which designate definite and easily recognizable objects or qualities. Table, for example, is an easily recognizable object and brown an easily recognizable quality. Such words are unambiguous. No serious doubts as to their meaning exist. The second class contains words which designate entities and qualities less definite and less easily recognizable. Some of these are highly abstract words, generalizing certain features of many highly complex situations. Such words as 'justice,' 'science,' 'society,' are examples. In the same class we must place the numerous words which designate psychological states — words such as 'beauty,' 'goodness,' 'spirit,' 'personality.' I have already mentioned the apparently irresistible human tendency to objectify psychological states and project them, on the wings of their verbal vehicle, into the outer world. Words like those I have just mentioned are typical vehicles of objectification. They are the cause of endless intellectual confusion, endless emotional distress, endless misdirections of voluntary effort.

Our third class contains words which are supposed to refer to objects in the outer world or to psychological states, but which in fact, since observation fails to reveal the existence of such objects or states, refer only to figments of the imagination. Examples of such words are the 'dragon' of the Chinese and the 'death instinct' of Freudian psychologists.

The most effective, the most psychologically magical words are found in the secondary category. This is only to be expected. Words of the second class are more ambiguous than any others and can therefore be used in an almost indefinite number of contexts. A recent American study has shown that the word 'nature' has been used by the philosophers of the West in no less than thirty-nine distinct senses. The same philosopher will give it, all unconsciously of course, three or four different meanings in as many paragraphs. Given such ambiguity, any thesis can be defended, any course of action morally justified, by an appeal to nature.

Ambiguity is not the only characteristic which makes these words peculiarly effective in determining conduct. Those which stand for generalizations and those which designate psychological states lend themselves, as we have already seen, to objectification. They take verbal wings and fly from the realm of abstraction into the realm of the concrete, from the realm of psychology into the external universe.

The objectification and even the personification of abstractions is something with which every political speech and newspaper article has made us familiar. Nations are spoken of as though they were persons having thoughts, feelings, a will and even a sex, which, for some curious reason, is always female. This female, personal nation produces certain psychological effects on those who hear it (or rather her) being talked about—effects incomparably more violent than those that would be produced if politicians were to speak about nations as what in fact they are: organized communities inhabiting a certain geographical area and possessing the means to wage war. This last point is crucially important. California is an organized community; but since it does not possess an army and navy, it cannot qualify for a place in the League of Nations.

Another familiar entity in political speeches is the pseudo-person called 'Society.' Society has a will, thoughts and feelings, but, unlike the Nation, no sex. The most cursory observation suffices to show that there is no such thing as Society with a large S. There are only very large numbers of individual societies, organized in different ways for different purposes. The issue is greatly complicated by the fact that the people who talk about this non-existent Society with a big S, tend to do so in terms of biological analogies which are, in many cases, wholly inapplicable. For example, the so-called philosophical historians insist on talking of a society as though it were an organism. In some aspects, perhaps, a society does resemble an organism. In others, however, it certainly does not. Organisms grow old and die and their component cells break down into inanimate substances. This does not happen to a society, though many historians and publicists loosely talk as though it did. The individuals who compose what is called a decadent or collapsed society do not break down into carbon and water. They remain alive; but the cells of a dead organism are dead and have ceased to be cells and become something else. If we want to talk about the decline and fall of societies in terms of scientific analogies, we had better choose our analogy from physics rather than biology. A given quantity of water, for example, will show least energy, more energy, most energy according to its temperature. It has most energy in the form of superheated steam, least in the form of ice. Similarly, a given society will exhibit much energy or little energy according to the way in which its individual members live their lives. The society of Roman Italy, for example, did not die; it passed from a high state of energy to a lower state of energy. It is for historians to determine the physiological, psychological, economic and religious conditions accompanying respectively a high and a low degree of social energy.

The tendency to objectify and personify abstractions is found not only among politicians and newspaper men, but also among those who belong to the, intellectually speaking, more respectable classes of the community. By way of example, I shall quote a paragraph from the address delivered by Clerk Maxwell to the British Association in 1873. Clerk Maxwell was one of the most brilliantly original workers in the whole history of physics. He was also what many scientists, alas, are not—a highly cultivated man capable of using his intelligence in fields outside his particular specialty. Here is what he could say before a learned society, when at the height of his powers.

"No theory of evolution," he wrote, "can be formed to account for the similarity of molecules." (Throughout this passage, Maxwell is using the word 'molecule' in the sense in which we should now use the word 'atom'.) "For evolution necessarily implies continuous change, and the molecule is incapable of growth or decay, of generation or destruction. None of the processes of Nature, from the time when Nature began, have produced the slightest difference in the properties of any molecule. We are therefore unable to ascribe either the existence of the molecules or the identity of their properties to any of the causes which we call natural. Thus we have been led along a strictly scientific path very near to the point at which Science must stop. . . . In tracing back the history of matter Science is arrested when she assures herself, on the one hand that the molecule has been made and, on the other, that it has not been made by any of the processes which we call natural."

The most interesting point that emerges from these lines is the fact that, like the Nation, but unlike Society, Science has a sex and is a female. Having recorded this item in our text books of natural history, we can go on to study the way in which even a mind of the calibre of Clerk Maxwell's can be led into absurdity by neglecting to analyze the words which it uses to express itself. The word 'science' is current in our everyday vocabulary. It can be spelt with a capital S. Therefore it can be thought of as a person; for the names of persons are always spelt with capital letters. A person who is called Science must, *ex hypothesi,* be infallible. This being so, she can pronounce without risk of contradiction, that "none of the processes of Nature, since the time when Nature began," (Nature is also spelt with a capital letter and is of course also a female) "have produced the slightest difference in the properties of any molecule." Twenty-three years after the date of Maxwell's speech, Becquerel observed the radioactivity of uranium. Two years after that Mme. Curie discovered radium. At the turn of the new century Rutherford and Soddy demonstrated the fact that the radium atom was in a process of rapid disintegration and was itself derived from uranium whose atoms were disintegrating at a much slower rate.

This cautionary story shows how fatally easy it is for even the greatest men of science to take the particular ignorance of their own time and place, and raise it to the level of a universal truth of nature. Such errors are particularly easy when words are used in the entirely illegitimate way in which Maxwell employed the word 'Science.' What Maxwell should have said was something like this, "Most Western scientists in the year 1873 believe that no process has ever modified the internal structure of individual atoms. If this is so (and of course the beliefs of 1873 may have to be modified at any moment in the light of new discoveries), then perhaps it may be legitimate to draw certain inferences of a theological nature regarding the creation of matter."

How was it possible, we may ask ourselves, that a man of Clerk

Maxwell's prodigious intellectual powers, should have committed a blunder so monstrously ridiculous, so obvious, when attention is called to it, to people of even the most ordinary mental capacities? The question demands a double answer — the first on the purely intellectual level, the second in terms of feeling and will. Let us deal with these in order. Maxwell made his mistake, first of all, out of a genuine intellectual confusion. He had accepted the English language without question or analysis, as a fish accepts the water it lives in. This may seem curious in the light of the fact that he had certainly not accepted the technical language of mathematics without question or analysis. We must remember, however, that non-technical language is picked up in infancy, by imitation, by trial and error, much as the arts of walking and rudimentary cleanliness are acquired. Technical languages are learned at a later period in life, are applied only in special situations where analysis is regarded as creditable and the ordinary habits of daily living are in abeyance. Children and young people must be deliberately taught to analyze the non-technical language of daily life. With very few exceptions, they will never undertake the task on their own initiative. In this respect, Maxwell was not exceptional. He turned his intensely original and powerful mind on to the problems of physics and mathematics, but never on those of everyday, untechnical language. This he took as he found it. And as he found in it such words as 'Science' with a capital S and a female sex, he made use of them. The results, as we have seen, were disastrous.

The second reason for Maxwell's error was evidently of an emotional and voluntary nature. He had been piously brought up in the Protestant tradition. He was also, as the few letters to his wife which have been printed seem to indicate, a practising mystic. In announcing that 'Science' with the capital S and the female sex had proved that atoms had not evolved, but had been created and kept unchangingly themselves by non-natural forces, he had a specifically religious purpose in view. He wanted to show that the existence of a demiurge after the pattern of Jehovah, could be demonstrated scientifically. And he wanted also, I suspect, to prove to himself that the psychological states into which he entered during his moments of mystical experience could be objectified and personified in the form of the Hebraic deity, in whose existence he had been taught to believe during childhood.

This brings us to the threshold of a subject, profoundly interesting indeed, but so vast that I must not even attempt to discuss it here; the subject of God and of the relations subsisting between that word and the external world of things and events, between that word and the inner world of psychological states. Shelley has sketched the nature of the problem in a few memorable sentences. "The thoughts which the word, 'God,' suggests to the human mind are susceptible of as many varieties as human minds themselves. The Stoic, the Platonist and the Epicurean, the Polytheist, the Dualist and the Trinitarian, differ infinitely in their conceptions of its meaning. . . . And not only has every sect distinct conceptions of the application of this name, but scarcely two individuals of the same sect, who exercise in any degree the freedom of their judgment, or yield themselves with any candour of feeling to the influencings of the visible world, find perfect coincidence of opinion to exist between them." Such, I repeat, is the problem. No complete solution of it is possible. But it can at least be very considerably clarified by anyone who is prepared to approach it armed with equipment suitable to deal with it. What is the nature of this suitable equipment? I would assign the first place to an adequate vocabulary. Students of religion have need of a language sufficiently copious and sufficiently analytical to make it possible for them to distinguish between the various types of religious experience, to recognize the difference between things and words, and to realize when they are objectifying psychological states and projecting them into the outside world.

Lacking such a language they will find that even a wide knowledge in the fields of theology, of comparative religion and of human behaviour will be of little use to them. It will be of little use for the simple reason that such knowledge has been recorded, up to the present time, in words that lend themselves to the maximum amount of intellectual confusion and the minimum of clarity and distinctness.

Words and their meanings—the subject is an enormous one. "Had we but world enough and time" as the poet says, we could continue our discussion of it almost indefinitely. But unfortunately, or perhaps fortunately, world and time are lacking, and I must draw to a close. I have been able in this place to let fall only a few casual and unsystematic remarks about those particular aspects of the science of signs which Charles Morris has called the semantic and pragmatic dimensions of general semiosis. I hope, however, that I have said enough to arouse an interest in the subject, to evoke in your minds a sense of its profound importance and a realization of the need to incorporate it systematically into the educational curriculum.

Any education that aims at completeness must be at once theoretical and practical, intellectual and moral. Education in the proper use of words is complete in the sense that it is not merely intellectual and theoretical. Those who teach, teach not only the science of signs, but also a universally useful art and a most important moral discipline. The proper use of language is an important moral discipline, for the good reason that, in this field as in all others, most mistakes have a voluntary origin. We commit intellectual blunders because it suits our interests to do so, or because our blunders are of such a nature that we get pleasure or excitement from committing them. I have pointed out that one of the reasons for Maxwell's really monstrous misuse of language must be sought in that great man's desire to reconcile his scientific ideas with the habits of religious belief he had contracted in childhood. There was a genuine confusion of thought; but a not entirely creditable wish was very definitely the father of this confusion. And the same is true, of course, about those who for propagandist purposes, personify such abstractions as 'Society' or 'the Nation.' A wish is father to their mistaken thought—the wish to influence their hearers to act in the way they would like them to act. Similarly, a wish is the father of the mistaken thought of those who allow themselves to be influenced by such preposterous abuses of language—the wish to be excited, to 'get a kick,' as the phrase goes. Objectified in the form of a person, the idea of a nation can arouse much stronger feelings than it can evoke when it is spoken of in more sober and accurate language. The poor fools who, as we like to think, are helplessly led astray by such machiavellian demogogues as Hitler and Mussolini are led astray because they get a lot of emotional fun out of being bamboozled in this way. We shall find, upon analysis, that very many of the intellectual errors committed by us in our use of words have a similar emotional or voluntary origin. To learn to use words correctly is to learn, among other things, the art of foregoing immediate excitements and immediate personal triumphs. Much self control and great disinterestedness are needed by those who would realize the ideal of never misusing language. Moreover, a man who habitually speaks and writes correctly is one who has cured himself, not merely of conscious and deliberate lying, but also (and the task is much more difficult and at least as important) of unconscious mendacity.

When Gotama insisted on Right Speech, when Jesus stressed the significance of every idle word, they were not lecturing on the theory of semiosis; they were inculcating the practice of the highest virtues. Words and the meanings of words are not matters merely for the academic amusement of linguists and logisticians, or for the aesthetic delight of poets; they are matters of the profoundest ethical significance to every human being.

AFTERWORD

It is pleasantly if fictionally fanciful to imagine Aldous Huxley pecking out the text for his essay *Words and Their Meanings*, sequestered in a stereotypic Hollywood studio bungalow. Clacking out a sentence here and a paragraph there, in between crafting dialogue for The Dream Factory, as Hortense Powdermaker later named the film colony. Nor is it much of a stretch to imagine the essay's message as one directed by Huxley at studio moguls who indentured the servitude (albeit well paid) of their studio talent. Then, the studio system bound screenwriters such as Huxley and other motion picture talent to seven-year contracts, renewable annually and with the right of first refusal resting exclusively with the studio. Huxley's disaffection for the system began with his first assignment at MGM. With veteran writer Jane Murfin, he collaborated on *Pride and Prejudice*, a process he described as "an odd, crossword puzzle job."

But far more likely than the scenario above, the essay seems a script for a salon-style soliloquy. An essay composed for the lecturer at a podium, delivered orally by reading the typescript verbatim. A manuscript voiced rather than extemporaneously presented, a rhetorical style that aligns exactly with the writer's message intentions. Word choice and precision matter, the essay makes clear. The text's arrangement is somewhat stiff and formal, a style better intended for the eye than the ear. Nevertheless, the not especially conversational presentation would have been received by an attentive audience at such Southern California book clubs as publisher Ward Ritchie's own Rounce & Coffin Club, or maybe the more prestigious Zamorano Club. The text is as disciplined, thoughtful, and precise as the argument Huxley makes. And the fact that The Ward Ritchie Press published several such titles (e.g., *America; a lecture*, April 13, 1939) supports the plausibility of the present thesis.

Words and Their Meanings was not Aldous Huxley's first experience with The Ward Ritchie Press. He wrote the foreword to *The*

Manuscripts of D. H. Lawrence, a 1937 title. Huxley arrived in Los Angeles that same year. The next year, Huxley's eight-page essay *The Most Agreeable Vice* (books and book collecting) was published for Jake Zeitlin in an edition of five hundred copies by Ritchie. Zeitlin, "the dean of Southern California booksellers," was a personal friend of Huxley's. While Huxley's and Ritchie's circles doubtless intersected and overlapped, exactly how the *Words* title came to be remains a bit of a mystery.

Ward Ritchie's book on his Press is mum on the subject (*The Ward Ritchie Press and Anderson, Ritchie & Simon*, Los Angeles, April 1961). Extant evidence is provocative but circumstantial. We know Huxley was no stranger to and among literary circles. He was also accustomed to being well compensated for his words: Huxley's 1939 salary when he joined MGM was an astonishing $1,000 a week, an incredible figure, especially for a previously "depression-proof" industry by then feeling the grip of the Depression. Few outside of the movie industry—never mind a private press such as Ritchie's—could have compensated him comparably.

But as Ritchie appreciatively noted, The Ward Ritchie Press had a well-known patron, maybe one among many, Delmer Daves. He was a "prime fairy godfather" of sorts. Best known today for directing 1950s westerns, Daves began his Hollywood career as a screenwriter, suggesting a professional commonality with Huxley. As significant, avocationally Daves possessed "the most agreeable vice" and was a book collector—one of Ward Ritchie Press's prime target audiences, as with virtually all private presses. And as a collector, perhaps Daves also might have facilitated, in one way or another, the publication of *Words*.

Alvin Lustig, the designer for *Words and Their Meanings*, briefly had ties to the Ritchie Press. Ward Ritchie met Lustig in 1937 and, shortly thereafter, Lustig moved into the Press's office space. They first collaborated on William van Wyck's *Robinson Jeffers* (1938). In 1940, Ritchie recalls, Lustig created "a dramatic cover" for a proposed book series, Scrapbook of Art. While a single title in the series was produced, "it just didn't sell," Ritchie wrote, "and the series died aborning." For Lustig, profiled in RIT Press's Graphic Design Archives Chapbook series (*Purity of Aim: The Book Jacket Designs of Alvin Lustig*, 2010), his "book covers are perhaps the most eloquent articulations of his vision for design in contemporary society." Ned Drew and Paul Sternberger describe Lustig's *Words* cover design, one his earliest, as "a stark juxtaposition of the author's signature, isolated for greater effect, and an abstract configuration of shapes, referring to the inherent complexities found in systems of writing and their organized syntax." Huxley's *Words* title is among three other works produced by Ritchie and designed by Lustig, and is mentioned only in passing and without further commentary in the Ritchie Press's history.

Words and Their Meanings was selected as "one of the Western Books of 1940," Ritchie reports. Begun in 1938, the Exhibition of Western Books was invented by Gregg Anderson, a partner beginning in 1935 in the Ritchie publishing enterprise. It was patterned after the Fifty Books of the Year Show of the American Institute of Graphic Arts, a celebration of fine printing. A redesigned edition of *Words* was printed in 1942. Ritchie's history offers no further details about this edition, and in neither case does Ritchie report the edition size, though one hundred copies of *Words* were specially printed for Zeitlin in May 1940.

Huxley is, unsurprisingly, carefully attuned and sensitive to words. His accomplishments in other media notwithstanding, as a Hollywood scribe he would be appreciative of the profound culturally and internationally influential medium that carried his own scripted words, though the worldwide window for American movies was closing quickly as more and more nations became engaged in the war.

The wider historical setting for *Words* includes an America still mired in a decade-deep, desperate economic depression, one incongruously counterpointed by Hollywood screwball comedies about the Great Depression, such as *My Man Godfrey* (1936), while anticipating the arrival of such reform-minded social problem films as *Sullivan's Travels* (1941) and the U.S. entry into World War II. The narrow intellectual context is formed by the contemporaneous mentalist-behavioral and linguistic relativity–determinism controversies. Huxley cites Charles W. Morris on this subject. Unstated, Huxley channels Morris's professor, George Herbert Mead and his discussion of signals, signs, and symbols (*Mind, Self, and Society*, 1934) and Sapir-Whorf. Huxley foresees Susanne Langer's discussion of language as presented in *Philosophy in a New Key* (1942). Despite lacking empirical support, the intuitive appeal of linguistic determinism remains today. Cumulatively, Huxley makes his case for "the psychological magic of words, their power to affect the thinking, feeling and behaviour of those who use them." Concluding, as would any good rhetorician, Huxley identifies his essay's future orientation, or what today we label a "call to action": "I hope . . . I have said enough to arouse an interest in the subject, to evoke in your minds a sense of its profound importance and a realization of the need to incorporate it systematically into the educational curriculum."

RIT Press acknowledges the permissions courtesies extended by the Aldous and Laura Huxley Literary Trust, Mark Trevenen

Huxley, and Teresa Huxley; Ward Ritchie, Jr.; and Elaine Lustig Cohen. We express our gratitude to our friend and longtime supporter Jon Budington for bringing to the Press's attention this fine essay and the opportunity to publish it.

Bruce A. Austin
Director, RIT Press
January 2018

COLOPHON

PRINTING
More Vang
Alexandria, VA

BINDING
Advantage Book Binding, Inc.
Baltimore, MD

DUST JACKET
Hahnemühle Bugra

TEXT PAPER
Mohawk Superfine Eggshell

TYPEFACES
Janson and Futura